MW00936523

Perfect Credit
In 12 Months

Perfect Credit In 12 Months

The Ultimate Guide to Fast Credit Repair

K N Carter

Copyright © 2016 K N Carter **All Rights Reserved.**
This publication is protected under the U.S. Copyright Act of 1976 and all
other applicable international, federal, state, and local laws. Any attempt to
reproduce, transmit, market or distribute this publication in part or in full
is strictly prohibited without the expressed written consent of the publisher.
The publisher warrants the content written is that of the author's discretion
and that content does not necessarily reflect the views and/or opinions of
the publisher in any capacity whatsoever. Your own circumstances may be
different than that of the author and therefore no representations or warran-
ties in regard to the use of this material is implied.
ISBN: 1456478206
ISBN 13:9781456478209

Acknowledgements

Special thanks to everyone who took the time to assist in the creation of this project and also to those of you who purchased this book as well.

The creation of this project manifested after I was able to go from having a **487 credit score after filing bankruptcy to a 771 credit score in under 1 year** using techniques I discovered through my own trial and error.

Initially, I started off with absolutely no credit. I applied for a few credit cards and eventually was able to get a card with a high interest rate and a $500 credit limit. I used the card responsibly and additional credit offers followed. In no time I obtained several mortgages to go along with my stack of credit cards. As time went on I amassed HUGE debts (nearly 1 million dollars) which overwhelmed me. I was stressed and soon came to the realization that I had dug a hole that I couldn't climb out of. Faced with many foreclosures and creditors calling every minute, I filed bankruptcy.

After filing bankruptcy, my credit score plummeted to 487. I attempted to apply for credit and was denied every single time. I began to research and try different methods. I discovered a formula I still use to this day. **In less than 12 months I was able to delete from my credit report- foreclosures, medical bills, a state tax lien, numerous delinquent credit accounts and even my bankruptcy!** I established new credit and within 1 year had a 771 FICO score. Now I want to share these techniques with you!

Table of Credit

Introduction

Whenever you make a purchase today with the promise to pay for it tomorrow, you are using credit. Before credit cards became so common, merchants had their own credit accounts. Our grandparents, or some parents, sometimes went to the store, picked up groceries for the week, and promised to pay the bill when they received their salary. The grocer was extending credit. If your grandparent always paid on time, the grocer might not have a problem letting them pick up more groceries. However, if your grandparent didn't settle the bill, the grocer might cut off the credit line and require your grandparent to pay for their groceries on the spot.

Credit has been standardized over the years and many stores belong to corporations that won't allow people to purchase goods unless they pay on the spot with cash, check, or a major credit card. No more promises to pay. Now big banks control whether you can use credit and how much you can use. Before a bank will allow you to use credit, it must first believe that you can be trusted to repay the amount of credit you use. This is considered financial trustworthiness.

Lenders use a number of factors to determine your financial trustworthiness and it's not based on how long they've known your family. Your credit history is one of the most commonly used factors. How you have used credit in the past – your credit history – is considered to be the best way to predict how you will use it in the future. Your credit history is reported in your credit report and measured by your credit score. Lenders also consider your income. Do you make enough money to pay back what you've borrowed? Even with a good history of repaying what you borrow, lenders want to know that you actually have (or will have) the means to pay back the credit you use. For new borrowers without a credit history, lenders may place more importance on your income. They may only give you a small amount of credit to start out with and increase your credit as you demonstrate you can handle it.

Some of us are very familiar with using credit and many of us also know all to well what it's like having terrible credit. As with anything in life, nothing worthwhile happens overnight or without effort. The same principles apply when rebuilding damaged or non-existing credit history. The following chapters have particularly been prepared to assist those with blemished credit by providing an understanding of the history of credit, ways to obtain credit, and techniques to maintain it.

One

What Are Credit Bureaus?

Credit reporting agencies or credit bureaus are part of a multi-billion dollar industry. According to Associated Credit Bureaus, Inc., a trade association of credit bureaus and mortgage reporting companies in the United States, the industry consist of nearly 680 credit bureaus, most of which are association members. Most credit bureaus are owned by or affiliated with one of the three national companies that dominate the industry (Experian, Equifax, and TransUnion) and are linked to their computer systems. These three companies are often referred to as "The Big Three." There are also smaller local or regional credit bureaus that have no relationship with the big three, as well as large national information brokers that purchase consumer credit information from the big three and resell that information to other businesses.

These national information brokers often maintain multiple databases with consumer credit information being just one of those databases.

The vast computerized libraries maintained by credit bureaus act as credit-related information clearinghouses on most American adults. Credit bureaus sell this information to retailers, credit card companies, insurance companies, banks, and other lending institutions. It is estimated that the big three update nearly 2 billion pieces of credit file information each month, received from thousands of businesses across the country, and generate more than 600 million consumer reports annually.

Information in Your Credit Record

A credit bureau maintains the information it collects on you in a credit record or file, which is actually a history of your use and management of credit.

Basic information in your credit file tells who has extended credit to you, whether you pay your bills on time, and how much you owe each of your creditors.

Where Do Credit Bureaus Get Their Information?

Credit reporting agencies obtain information about you from four basic sources: *subscribers, collection agencies, public records, and you.* Credit bureaus update their information regularly to provide a month-to-month profile of your use of credit.

In most instances, credit bureaus subscribers are companies that extend credit to consumers. They provide credit bureaus with information on the bill-paying habits of their account holders. Many credit bureaus require their subscribers to provide them with consumer account information on a monthly basis. Increasingly, creditors are using computers to relay consumer account information to credit reporting agencies, but some creditors continue to use manual methods.

Some collection agencies provide credit bureaus with information on accounts that are in collection.

Public records, the third source of credit bureau information, include bankruptcy filings, tax liens, and judgments. This information also appears on your credit report.

You are the fourth source of the data gathered and maintained by the credit bureaus. When you fill out a credit application, you list identifying information, such as your name, current and former addresses, age, and Social Security number. This information becomes a part of your credit file.

Who Sees Your Credit Report?

A credit report is an extremely important document because it contains information that can affect many aspects of your life. Among other things, your credit record can influence your ability to obtain new or additional credit and the terms of that credit as well as the job you have, especially if you will be responsible for handling or overseeing money. Credit report information may also affect your ability to get adequate insurance or to rent or buy a home.

The FCRA specifies who may review your credit report and for what purposes. According to the law, access to your credit file is limited to the following:

Potential creditors: Creditors may access consumer credit records to decide whether to extend credit, to review an account, or to collect a debt.

Potential insurers: Insurers may access consumer credit records for information that will assist them in the underwriting of an insurance policy.

Employers: Consumer credit reports are made available to employers or potential employers to help them make decisions regarding hiring, firing, reassignment, or promotion.

Potential investors, loan servicers, and current insurers: These businesses can use consumer credit information to value or assess the risks associated with an existing obligation.

Local, state, and federal agencies: This may include law enforcement officials, child support agencies, the IRS.

Others: Anyone may review your credit report if you give them written permission to do so.

Additionally, your credit record may be reviewed if someone gets a court order to do so; IRS subpoenas that information; or someone has a legitimate business need in connection with a business transaction you initiate. This includes the purchase of goods or services for your personal, family, or household use.

Insurers
Under the FCRA, insurers may review your credit record before granting you insurance. Some companies use the information in credit records to screen out high risk applicants. Others use it to determine whether to give someone who is already insured additional coverage, to raise that person's insurance rate, or to terminate coverage altogether.

Employers
If you apply for a job with a new employer or for a promotion with your current employer, the employer can review a copy of your credit record as part of the screening process. Your current employer can also read your credit file as

part of the process for deciding whether to take an adverse action against you-firing you perhaps. However, the FCRA says that before the employer can look at your credit record information, you must give your written permission to do so.

Furthermore, before the employer can purchase your credit report, it must certify certain things in writing to the credit bureau selling it. Among other things, it must certify that it has told you in writing that it may review your credit record as part of its decision-making process and that you have a right to obtain a copy of your report.

Credit bureaus will not provide an employer certain kinds of consumer credit record information such as the consumer's age, marital status, and account numbers for example.

If you do not get a job or promotion or if your current employer takes adverse action against you as a result, in whole or in part due to information in your credit file, the employer must provide you with a copy of the credit report it reviewed along with information about your rights under the FCRA, including information about how to correct credit record problems. However, even if you contend that there are inaccuracies in your file, the employer still can deny you the job or promotion, or take adverse action against you. This is a good argument for the importance of reviewing your credit record on a regular basis and clearing up any problems you may find in it.

The employer must also provide you with the name, address, and telephone number of the credit reporting agency that generated the credit report. It must also give you the credit bureaus toll-free phone number, assuming that the agency maintains information on consumers nationwide.

Government Agencies

Any government agency may review your credit record for purposes of granting credit, hiring, or insuring. Government agencies may also review your credit file if you are being considered for special license or a security clearance. For cases in which the law requires that your financial status or financial responsibility be reviewed, a government agency may use the information in your file to help determine your eligibility for a government benefit, including eligibility for welfare benefits. In addition, as a consequence of the 1996 amendments to the FCRA, the FBI is now allowed to access consumer credit reports in connection with an investigation.

Other than the specific purposes listed above, a government agency may access only identifying information from a credit report, such as your name, address, and the name of your employer.

Legitimate Need

Before the 1996 amendments to the FCRA, the law allowed anyone with a legitimate business need to gain access to a consumer's credit file. The FCRA did not define this term, which created a major loophole that credit reporting agencies used to their financial advantage. By interpreting the term legitimate business need broadly, the agency turned consumer credit information into a profitable commodity. Many use the consumer information in their databases to develop new products and services not directly related to the extension of credit.

During the early 1990s, consumer advocates attacked the buying and selling of consumer credit data as a violation of consumer privacy. They pointed out that when consumers provided information in their credit files, they assume the information will be used only to evaluate the credit worthiness. The consumer advocates also pointed out that credit bureaus are not required to remunerate consumers for the money they make buying and selling their credit record information.

States attorney generals and the Federal Trade Commission responded to this criticism by taking a closer look at the buying and selling of consumer credit record information and the FTC placed specific restrictions on the activity. In addition, under pressure from the FTC, Experian and Equifax stopped developing and selling targeted marketing lists derived from consumer credit record account data. TransUnion decided to fight the FTC with a lawsuit over its right to sell target marketing lists. If successful following litigation, all bureaus will be able to continue marketing activities.

Credit Bureau Security

A company must meet certain standards to become a credit bureau subscriber and prove the legitimacy of their business. Often, someone from the credit bureau will actually visit the business to verify its existence. These security measures help protect credit bureau information from being accessed by companies that intend to use it for unauthorized purposes.

Once a company is accepted as a subscriber, they receive a special code and security number, both of which are part of the system that credit agencies must have to help prevent unauthorized disclosure of data in their files. Companies must provide credit bureaus with its security code and number when requesting information about your credit history.

Though security measures exist, they have been known to fail. Therefore when reading your credit report, take note of the companies who have reviewed your file. Every time a request is made to review your file, it will show up in your credit report as an inquiry. Pay close attention to all the companies or organizations that have made an inquiry into your file. If you do not recognize them contact the bureau, as this could be an indication of unauthorized use.

Investigative Reports

Credit reporting agencies sometimes provide investigative reports to other companies, mainly insurance providers and potential employers. Most consumers are not familiar with these reports because Members of Associated Credit Bureaus, Inc. rarely constructs this type of report. Reports such as these contain subjective information about consumers like details about personal habits, lifestyle decisions, and overall character. Prior to a company obtaining an investigative report on a consumer, it must provide the consumer written notification of its request no later than three days after the company first asks a credit bureau to prepare the report. It must also inform the consumer of his or her rights under the FCRA provisions covering investigative reports. Furthermore, before the credit bureau can prepare the investigative report, the company must provide a written explanation as to why it wants the report and certify in writing that it will not misuse the information in the report for any other purpose and that it has provided the consumer with the aforementioned notifications. The company must also certify that a complete and accurate disclosure of the nature of its investigation will be provided to the consumer upon request.

Amendments to the FCRA further protect consumers by requiring the verification of the accuracy of any investigative report containing any public record information relating to a consumer's arrest, indictment, conviction, tax lien, outstanding judgment, etc. The FCRA bars a credit bureau from including in the report any negative personal information about a consumer that it obtains from the consumer's friends or associates without first trying to corroborate the facts through other sources.

Any application you submit for credit which is denied as a result of information about you in an investigative report, the law requires the company that requested the report to provide you with the name, address, and phone number of the credit bureau that prepared the report as well as written notification of your right to obtain a free copy of the report and your right to dispute any information that you do not agree with.

Months 1-3

Obtain a copy of your credit report from each of the major credit bureaus and examine them thoroughly. Correct any typos or incorrect information by submitting the correct information to the appropriate bureau.

Given that your credit record can span over a long period of time, it is likely that your credit reports contain some errors. Some common credit reporting mistakes include out-of-date addresses, closed accounts being shown as open, and outright false information.

Dispute all errors. Since you will want your credit score to be an accurate representation of your credit history and credit worthiness, you will need to make sure the reports that your credit scores are based on are accurate. A Federal Trade Commission study found that 25 percent of credit reports could contain errors that impact scores.

Insider Secret
Deny everything.

    When it comes to accounts that damage your credit score such as parking tickets, medical bills, or a balance from an old cell phone, it makes sense to dispute them with all the credit bureaus. Since the debts are usually older and small, the companies and creditors will most likely not even bother going through the hassle to respond to your dispute. Therefore by denying their existence or requesting validation during the dispute process, chances are some negative items will be forever deleted from your credit report.

TWO

Credit Report Basics
Requesting a Copy of Your Credit Report

There are a number of ways to request a copy of your credit report from one of the big three such as:

1. Visit www.freeannualcreditreport.com (every American is entitled to 1 free credit report from each of the big three on an annual basis).
2. Send the credit bureau a request letter
3. Order by phone using the credit bureaus automated credit report request system (You may be charged a fee for this service).
4. Order an online copy of your credit report (You may be charged a fee for this service).

To avoid delays in processing your credit report requests from Equifax, Experian, and Trans Union, it's always best to call their customer service department or to visit their websites listed below:

1. Experian- www.experian.com
2. Equifax- www.equifax.com
3. TransUnion- www.transunion.com

These websites offer a lot of helpful information and advice about credit and identity theft protection.

Writing a Letter to Request a Copy of Your Credit Report

When you write a letter to obtain a copy of your credit report, you must include very specific information. Type your name, and be sure to include any suffix such as "Jr.," "Sr.," "III," and so forth when applicable. Also include your date of birth, Social Security number, current address and former address if you have not been at your current address for at least five years, and the name of your current employer. Include your spouse's name if you're married and your daytime and evening phone numbers with area codes. Send along a copy of a billing statement from a major credit card, a utility bill, your driver's license or any document that reflects your current address to help the credit reporting agency verify for security purposes that you are in fact the person requesting the copy of your credit report. Finally, be sure to sign your letter so the credit bureau has your signature on file; it too is needed for security purposes.

If you are writing to a credit bureau because you have been denied credit, insurance, or employment within the past 60 days because of the information about you that the bureau is maintaining, you will not have to pay anything for a copy of your credit report. However, be sure that you include with the letter you send a copy of the denial letter you received from the creditor, insurer, or employer that reviewed your credit file. If on the other hand you are writing to the credit bureau because you want to know what is in your credit record and to review it for errors, be sure to enclose a check or money order for the appropriate amount.

Where to Send Your Letter When You are Requesting a Copy of Your Credit Report from One of the Big Three.

Instructions for ordering a copy of your credit report will vary depending on the reason you are ordering it: You have been denied credit, employment, or insurance because of the information in your credit record or in an investigative report, or you want to review your report to make sure it contains no errors or omissions. Special ordering instructions may apply for residents of certain states. You can learn if your state is one of them by contacting the bureaus listed below:

Send your request letter to:

Experian
PO Box 949
Allen, TX 75013-0949
1-888-397-3742
www.experian.com

TransUnion
P.O. Box 1000
Chester, PA 19016
(800) 888-4213
www.transunion.com

Equifax
PO Box 740241
Atlanta, GA 30374-0241
1-800-685-1111
www.equifax.com

If You Have Been Denied Credit, Employment, or Insurance

If you are ordering a copy of your credit report because you have been denied credit, employment, or insurance as a result to information contained in your credit record or in an investigative report, under the FCRA you are entitled to receive a free copy of either report from the credit bureau that prepared it. The company that denied you credit, employment, or insurance must give you the name and address of the credit bureau that provided the negative information. To get your free report, you must request it within 60 days of your denial.

What's in a Credit Report?

All credit reports include the same basic types of information: an identification number, identifying data, credit history, inquiries, and public record information. Each credit reporting agency uses a different format for presenting this information.

If you do not understand some of the information in your credit report, call the credit bureau that generated it for explanations. The FCRA requires the credit bureau that generated your report to have personnel available who can help you. Your report should include either a toll-free number to call or the address or phone number of an affiliated bureau.

Identifying Data
The identifying information in your credit report usually includes the following:

1. Name, including any nicknames you may have used and whether you are a junior, senior, III, IV and so on.
2. Current and previous addresses
3. Birth date

4. Spouse's name
5. Current and previous employers
6. Social Security number

This information generally comes from credit and loan applications that you have filled out.

Credit History

The heart of any credit report is the payment history on accounts that were reported to the credit agency. Despite the slightly different credit report formats used by each credit bureau, most reports reflect the following types of account information:

- Name of the creditor and account/ loan number
- Nature of the account (whether it is joint or individual)
- Type of account/loan- revolving, installment, student loan, mortgage, etc.
- Date account or loan was opened
- Credit limit on account/ loan amount
- Current balance on account/loan
- Monthly payment amount
- Account payment history, including the number of late payments and whether an account has been referred to collections or has been closed by the consumer or the creditor.
- Date information on the account/loan was last reported

- Number of months for which information has been reported
- Amount of credit that has been extended to the consumer

Inquiries

The inquiries section of a credit report indicates those creditors and others who have checked your credit file for any reason. Some of the inquires listed will be preceded by such abbreviations as *PRM*, *AM*, and *AR*. PRM indicates that the inquiry was made for *promotional* purposes- your credit file was reviewed or screened for a preapproved credit offer. AM stands for account monitoring and AR for account review, both of which mean that one of your creditors reviewed the information in your file, perhaps to determine whether your line of credit should be increased or your credit card canceled. The only inquiries that are reported to businesses when they review the information in your credit file are those that result from your application for new or additional credit.

The FCRA does not specify the maximum amount of time that an inquiry can or should remain on a credit report, but it does indicate the minimum amount of time that an inquiry should stay there. That minimum is two years for employment purposes and six months for all other purposes.

Although the inquiries section of a credit report may seem relatively unimportant, it can have a significant bearing on your ability to get credit because lenders consider the number of credit-related inquiries in your file to be an indicator of how much credit you are trying to obtain. If lenders see a lot of inquiries, they may assume that you are applying for too much credit and will not be a responsible user of credit, and they are therefore likely to deny your credit request.

The FCRA does not provide consumers any rights with regard to inquiries. Regardless, it is always a good idea to challenge any inquiries that you do not recognize as the reporting agency may be willing to investigate them for you.

Public Record Information

The information in this section of a credit report refers to credit-related events that are a matter of public record such as bankruptcies, foreclosures, judgments, and tax liens. The public information section may also make note of convictions. In an effort to reduce the number of parents who are falling behind or totally ignoring their child support payments, state or local agencies that enforce child support agreements are beginning to report child support delinquencies to credit bureaus.

What Your Credit Report Says about You

After you receive a copy of your credit report, you'll probably be surprised to discover what is and isn't in the report and that it may be incomplete. Your credit record is not a truly comprehensive portrait of you as a consumer for a number of reasons. First, all credit reporting agencies do not get their consumer credit information from the same subscribers. Therefore, no credit bureau will have a comprehensive history of your use of credit. Second, not every creditor maintains an ongoing subscriber relationship with every credit reporting agency and thus does not regularly report consumer account information to every credit bureau. In fact, some creditors may only provide credit record information to a credit bureau when a consumer account is in collection or in default. Auto dealers, mortgage companies, department stores and local retailers, utilities companies, and medical providers all tend to work this way.

When you review your credit report, you may find that it does not reflect significant account information but that information you would rate as relatively unimportant is in your credit file. For example, unless you have ever been 90 days late or more on your mortgage payment, your payment history on that loan will probably not be reflected in your credit history. Yet for most consumers a mortgage is the single largest financial commitment they make! On the other hand, the fact that you may have been a couple of days late with a small monthly bankcard payment will most likely appear in your report.

Three

If knowing how to read your credit report isn't all that high on your list of priorities, you may want to rethink that. Since your personal credit report represents the standard by which all banks, lending institutions and other financial entities measure your overall credit worthiness or in the simplest terms, your ability to pay back loans, understanding your personal credit report is crucial.

Your personal credit report is broken down into six (6) main sections:

1. **Personal information** – This area lists all available information about you, including your date of birth, where you currently live and past addresses plus

other personal details such as your current employer. There is also a sub-section for consumer statements. Consumer statements can be included in your credit report. They represent your chance to explain a particular credit discrepancy, problem, or issue. If you choose to add a consumer statement to your credit report, you can do so by contacting any of the three major U.S. credit bureaus directly -TransUnion, Experian and Equifax.

2. **(Credit) Account summary** - This is an at-a-glance summary of your entire account history, and it shows active/open and inactive/closed accounts in your name, as per the three main credit bureaus. NOTE: The public records section is usually marked "0" (for zero) unless you have ever declared bankruptcy, had a home foreclosure or had anything in your credit report information history that has become a matter of public record.

3. **Personal payment history** – This section details your payment history for all credit accounts. You'll see mortgages, or real estate accounts, installment and revolving credit accounts (such as credit cards), accounts in collection and any other accounts in your name all as they relate to each of the three credit bureaus.

4. **Public information** - Like the public records notation in your account summary, this section provides specifics on anything in your overall credit

report information that is a matter of official public record such as bankruptcies, tax liens, foreclosures and any other legal actions relating to your personal credit.

5. **Inquiries** – This area lists businesses and agencies that have inquired about your credit during the last two years. For instance, when you apply for credit, the lender will submit an "inquiry" to each of the credit bureaus about your overall credit history.

6. **Creditor contacts** – Here you'll find contact information such as mailing address, phone number or website address for all of your current creditors.

How often do I need to check my credit report?

The biggest problem many consumers seem to have is ignoring their credit report altogether, only paying attention when they are turned down for a loan or they find they have difficulty getting a mortgage. For that reason, you should check your credit on a regular basis and there has never been more information available to do just that. Not only is it your legal right to request a copy of your credit report at any time (either through the mail or via an online credit report), there are also a variety of services that offer credit report monitoring. Such services automatically alert you to any changes in your credit report. It is then up to you to investigate the specific issue, problem or discrepancy.

Will my credit scores vary by individual credit bureaus?

The simple answer is "yes." Your credit scores may vary only slightly, or they may vary by 100 points or more. While you're entitled by law to receive a free credit report each year from each of the three main credit bureaus, these reports do not include your scores. Plus, each report is, by nature, a single-bureau credit report providing you with only one-third of your complete and updated credit information.

Also, if you only check your credit report once a year you won't stay up-to-date on your credit score for 12 months which can leave you without an effective tool for determining the best time to apply for a mortgage or car loan. Beyond that, you may not be aware of unauthorized changes to your credit report that can adversely affect your score and provide an early sign of a risk of identity theft.

While most incorrect information on your credit report should be disputed with the credit bureaus directly, personal information such as your name, address or employment information can be corrected through your creditors. Simply ask them to update your records and they'll send the new information with their monthly update to the credit bureaus.

Keep in mind that your credit is tied to your Social Security number and not disputing incorrect personal details won't necessarily impact your credit health. Your credit doesn't need your latest address to keep developing. It's far more important to dispute incorrect account information on your credit report.

When checking out the accounts listed on your credit report, ensure that your lenders are properly reporting your activity and watch for accounts you didn't open. Remember that creditors aren't required to report to every bureau, so if you're missing an account, first check with your lender to see which bureau(s) they report to.

In the credit inquiries section, make sure you recognize each hard inquiry listed. If you don't, it could indicate that someone is applying for credit in your name. You may also want to dispute inquiries that are still on your report after two years.

Lastly, look through each negative item (public records and accounts in collections), and make sure all the information, like the current status and date reported is correct. Paying off your account in collections and negotiating with the collection agency to mark it as "paid in full" or "settled" could lessen the negative impact on your score; therefore, it's worth ensuring this particular detail is up to date.

The bottom line: Your credit report isn't a complicated monster that you need to fear. Since your credit score is based on your report, take the time to ensure that your report is free of errors so that your score accurately represents you.

Four

Credit Record Problems

No firm number exists to show the percentage of credit files that have problems. It is estimated to be as high as 50 percent but given industry efforts to reduce that rate, the percentage may be lower today. In addition, some of the amendments to the FCRA are intended to further reduce the incidence of credit record problems. Realistically, however, given that the industry collects more than 2 billion pieces of credit-related information each month and generates more than 600 million credit reports on close to 200 million consumers every year, there are bound to be errors in some credit files. Credit bureaus do make mistakes. Also, sometimes creditors and other information providers give credit bureaus incorrect information. Therefore, to protect yourself, read your credit report very carefully.

Common Credit Record Errors Include The Following:

- Information is commingled. Your credit record includes credit information for someone with a name similar or identical to yours.
- The name of a former spouse appears on your credit record.
- Your name is misspelled, your address is wrong, or your Social Security number is incorrect.
- Duplicate accounts show up
- Account information is inaccurate or incomplete.
- Outdated information is included
- Account information does not relate to you.
- Unauthorized inquiries are listed.

Correcting Problems in Your Credit Report

If you find information in your credit report that you believe is inaccurate, complete the dispute form that will come with your report. Follow the form's instructions for filling it out.

You may also want to attach a letter to your completed form, dated and signed by you, along with copies of any documentation you have that helps prove the error in your report. The documentation might include copies of canceled checks, receipts, account statements, or previous correspondence between you and the creditor involved. Or if the lien the IRS placed on your property has been released because you paid off your back taxes but your credit record still shows the lien, enclose a copy of the document that released the lien.

Attaching a letter to the dispute form is a good idea if you don't think the credit bureau's form gives you adequate space to explain why you think there is an error in your report.

Keep a copy of your completed dispute form, letter, and backup documentation to provide you with a record of what you said and when you said it. Also, the date of the letter will let you know when you should have heard back from the credit bureau. The FCRA says that after you've contacted a credit bureau about a problem in your credit record, it must respond to you within 30 days of receiving your dispute request form.

The third reason for sending a letter along is that if legal action becomes necessary, copies of what you sent to the bureau will help create a written record of exactly what steps you took and information you provided in order to clear up the problem.

Once you have completed the credit dispute form, mail it, your letter, and copies of any documentation you may have to the address on the form. Send it by certified mail with a request for return receipt. When you get the signed receipt back, file it with the rest of your credit record information.

What to Include in Your Letter

When you write your letter explain clearly what is wrong with your credit report and attach a copy of the report to your letter. Highlight or circle each of the problems you want corrected.

Include in your letter, in addition to the above, the same identification information you must include in a credit report request letter-your full name, current address, Social Security number, and so forth.

Recordkeeping

Set up an easy to follow recordkeeping system to help monitor the status of your disputes with creditors and/or any of the credit bureaus and to help organize materials related to the credit reporting issue(s).

Make copies of all the documents related to the issue that you send and receive, and keep them stored in a folder. If you happen to have a telephone conversation regarding the issue, keep a record of that discussion, including the date and time of the call as well as the name of the person to whom you spoke with and what was said.

Other things to keep in your recordkeeping system include receipts relating to any cost you may have incurred trying to resolve the credit reporting issue, account statements, and your credit report. In addition, if you ever take time off from work to do something related to the credit reporting issue, make a note of the date, the purpose of the errand, and the length of time you took off.

Good recordkeeping will not only help you monitor what is happening with an investigation into your dispute; it also creates a written record that may be used in the future if you ever have to pursue legal action against a credit bureau or file a formal complaint with the Federal Trade Commission (FTC).

Frivolous or Irrelevant Investigations

A credit bureau can refuse to conduct an investigation if it is determined that your request is frivolous or irrelevant. However, you must be notified in writing about the decision and reasons must be provided as to why they think your request is frivolous or irrelevant. The credit bureau must also tell you about what you are required to provide if an investigation is to occur.

The Credit Bureau's Response

The FCRA provides that within five business days of receiving your investigation request, the credit bureau must contact the provider of the information you are disputing and ask that its accuracy be checked. The information provider must then respond by verifying to the credit bureau that the information is either correct or incorrect.

Even though the credit bureau must complete its investigation within 30 days of receiving your request, if you provide the credit bureau with additional information relevant to the investigation during the 30 day time period, the credit bureau has the right to extend its investigation for up to 15 days. This does not apply if the credit bureau has already determined that the information you are disputing is inaccurate.

The Outcome of an Investigation

The credit bureau must send you written notice of its findings within five business days of completing it investigation. If it has been determined that the information you are disputing is an error or if the information cannot be verified, the information must be deleted from your credit record or your credit record must be immediately modified to reflect the correct information. However, if it is later determined that the information you disputed is accurate, the information can be reinserted into your credit file. If corrections are made to your credit file, be sure to periodically monitor your credit report. That way you can be sure the problem you thought had been corrected has not reappeared due to a clerical error or computer glitch.

Outdated or Inaccurate Information That Reappears in Your Credit Report

Consumers often discover that the information they thought had been corrected or deleted later reappears in their credit files. Sometimes this is because the credit bureau subsequently receives proof from the provider of the information that the information being disputed was in fact accurate. Other times it is due in part to human error.

In order to help address the problem, the FCRA now requires credit reporting agencies to maintain "reasonable procedures designed to prevent the reappearance of deleted information." Because the law does not define "reasonable procedures" however, the actual impact of this new provision has yet to be seen. On the other hand, the revised law also says that before deleted information can be reinserted into your credit file, the information provider must certify in writing to the credit bureau that the information is indeed accurate and complete. Furthermore, the credit bureau must notify you in writing, within five business days, that the information has been reinserted.

When a Disputed Credit Report Problem is not Corrected after an Investigation

Often times a credit bureau's investigation will find that the information you are disputing is correct. If this is the case, you have several options. One option is to locate new or additional documentation to help support your case. Make copies of any such documentation, write the credit bureau, and staple everything together. Make sure you make a copy of the letter for your files and send the information via certified mail with a request for a return receipt.

Another option is to contact the company that provided the information you are disputing and ask that they correct the problem. Prepare a letter similar to the one you mailed to the credit bureau and include with it copies of all information. In your letter, ask that the creditor send a correction request to all of the credit bureaus it reports to as well as to you. Also, ask the company to direct the credit bureaus to correct your credit file.

A third option for resolving a credit record problem is to call your state Attorney General's office of consumer affairs to see if they can help you. Many states have their own credit reporting laws.

Written Statements

If you are notified by a credit bureau that the information you are disputing is correct, they must also tell you about your fourth option- preparing a written statement of no more than 100 words for your credit file. Use the statement to explain why you believe the information in your credit file is incorrect. By law your statement must become a permanent part of your credit file and must be provided to anyone who reviews your credit report.

Insider Secret
"Bribe Em"

They say you shouldn't bribe anyone, but that is a term used loosely for consumers who negotiate "payment for deletion". If you have missed enough payments to have an account in collections, creditors will often agree to erase any negative credit reporting for that account if you pay it off in full. Make sure you get the agreement in writing. Collection companies more than likely will settle for a smaller lump sum payment because they purchased the debt from your original creditor for pennies on the dollar.

Months 4-6

Mentally prepare to change your spending habits. Do not utilize too much credit. Whenever possible, it's best to avoid racking up too much debt on your credit cards. Instead, try using less than 15 percent of your total credit limits. This shows lenders that you are responsibly using your cards and that you are not dependent on them for everyday purchases.

Monitor your score closely. It's hard to improve your score without knowing what it is and how it's being affected. Monitoring your credit doesn't have to cost you money. Free credit monitoring services allow you to easily track your score over time and see the fluctuations that could signal significant changes to your credit.

Five

Rebuilding your Credit

A lot changes when you lose your credit. The most notable difference is that you have to live on a cash basis, which usually means making difficult choices about how to spend your limited dollars. When you lose your credit, you cannot turn to credit cards when you've used up your paycheck!

Often, people who no longer have credit and who have to rely on themselves begin to reassess their values and priorities. They asked themselves what they really want out of life, how important spending and material possessions are to them, and whether those things are so important that they will use credit to get these possessions. They also begin thinking about sacrificing and saving for things they really need or want.

Reassessing priorities is an important conversation to have with yourself if your credit history has been seriously damaged and you can now begin to rebuild your credit. From my experience some people who file for bankruptcy or get into serious financial difficulty shared a common pattern: their desires for change exceeded their ability to pay, and they began using credit to immediately fulfill their every desire. These people failed to distinguish between what they needed and what they wanted and between what they could save for future purchases and what needs to be purchased with credit. Many of them tried to get as much credit as possible and then used it, whether they could make the payments or not.

As a rule, consumers who can distinguish between their needs and their desires, who can delay using credit except when absolutely necessary, and who are willing to sacrifice to get what they want are less apt to develop serious money problems. Credit is not something you use to make all your dreams come true. Credit is a tool you can use to purchase something really important when you have no other practical way of paying for it.

Why having credit may be necessary

Although there are arguments for living without credit and it can certainly be done, in today's world that's not always practical. Not having credit will make buying a house or other major items more difficult, and it can also mean that you won't be able to obtain a loan to help finance your children's college education. This may not be a problem for those of you who don't consider owning a house or buying a new car a desire or even a necessity. And some of you will no doubt decide that you're going to place most of the financial burden for your children's education on them, not on yourself. But those of you who don't share these beliefs, you will probably want to be able to obtain new credit eventually at reasonable terms.

A sound approach to credit rebuilding

To avoid getting into trouble again, strictly limit the amount of credit you apply for, shop for the best deal possible, and get credit only for a specific purpose. In other words, don't get credit just to have credit. That means no more multiple bank cards or multiple bank credit lines. You don't need them and having them will only tempt you.

If you want to buy a home, don't focus on rebuilding and obtaining credit for that specific purpose. The same holds true for cars and other big-ticket items. The key to successful credit rebuilding is gaining the trust of your creditors, and you'll have to do that the old-fashioned way-earn it. You must prove to potential creditors that despite your past money troubles and regardless of why those troubles developed, in the future you will manage your money wisely and pay all of your debts on time.

I recommend that you begin rebuilding trust at the local level, in your own community. That's where you should focus your efforts to get new credit. You have a better chance of rebuilding when potential creditors can meet you face-to-face, are familiar with where you work, may know your family, or attend your same church. Now let's talk about how to rebuild your credit.

When to start rebuilding your credit

Once the financial difficulties that contributed to your credit history problems are behind you, you can start rebuilding your credit. Usually however, if you file for bankruptcy, you have to wait until your bankruptcy has concluded. Generally, you can start rebuilding 6 to 10 months after its conclusion, although your bankruptcy will remain in your credit record for up to 10 years.

To prepare for getting new credit, the following are some things you need to do first:

Review your credit record with each of the big three credit bureaus to spot errors, missing positive account information, or accurate negative information that you feel merits an explanation.

Correct any errors you find and add written statements as necessary.

Begin saving each month, even if it's only a small amount. Having a financial cushion will help you resist the temptation to use credit in the future.

Keep trouble-free any credit account you may still have.

Develop good money management skills. Your local consumer credit counseling service office, a nearby college or university, a county extension service, and the like are all possible sources of help.

The credit rebuilding process

During the rebuilding process you should keep in mind a number of important rules of thumb. First, the credit rebuilding process will take time, so don't get impatient. Second, don't be fooled into thinking that you can speed up the process with the help of a credit repair firm. You'll be wasting your money when you work with one of these firms because they can't do anything you can't do for yourself for free. Third, keep to a minimum the amount of credit you apply for. One national bank card is really all you really need as most restaurants, retailers, and other consumer-oriented businesses accept either MasterCard or Visa cards. Having multiple bank cards may be too tempting, and as a result you may take on too much debt. Furthermore, potential creditors will be less inclined to extend you credit if they see that you already have a lot of bankcards. Incidentally, you will probably have to start with a secured national bankcard, but once you've established a credit history of responsible payments on the secured card, apply for an unsecured bankcard.

Most local and regional retailers accept cards issued by Visa, MasterCard, or both, so most charge cards issued by stores unnecessarily and usually have relatively high interest rates.

Set a goal of paying off your bankcard in full each month. If that is sometimes not possible, don't charge more on the card until you've paid off all existing charges.

As I've already suggested, concentrate on building credit in your own community. For example, save money with a local bank. Once you have between $500 and $1000 in your savings account, apply to the bank for a small loan secured with the funds in your savings account. If the bank where you have your account is unwilling to make you that loan, apply for a cash secured loan with other banks in your area.

After you've paid off the first bank loan apply for second small loan that is not cash secured. You may also want to apply to your bank for a secured credit card.

The process I just described is not the only way to rebuild a damaged credit history, but it is one that has worked well for my associates and I. What is best for you will depend on your previous credit history and your present circumstances.

Remember, however, that regardless of how you rebuild your credit, the goal is not to get all the credit you can but to get only the credit you really need.

Getting a bank loan

When you are ready to apply for a loan, call and schedule an appointment with a consumer loan officer at your bank. Explain over the phone that you have had money troubles, have damaged or blemished credit, and would like to discuss in person the possibility of getting a cash secured loan.

If the loan officer tells you over the phone that he or she is not interested in working with you because of your credit history, call other banks in your community. Continue calling banks until you find a loan officer willing to at least meet with you to discuss your needs. If the bank where you have your savings and/or checking accounts is not willing to work with you, then you should try banks in your community that are actively promoting debt consolidation loans or try the bank where your employer banks. If your employer has banked there for a long time and is a valued customer, the bank may be willing to work with you, especially if your employer provides a reference letter. Credit unions are another option.

Banks and loan officers

Banks are highly regulated businesses. They are expected to minimize the risks they take lending and investing money to safeguard their depositors' funds. In fact, if a bank makes too many high risk loans, it may lose its character and be out of business.

The career of a loan officer is in large part influenced by the success of the loans the officer makes. A loan officer who makes lots of loans that perform well, loans that are paid off on schedule, is much more likely to have a successful career at a bank than one who makes lots of loans that perform poorly. It's understandable therefore that with a damaged credit history, you are not going to be as attractive to a loan officer as someone with an unblemished record. As a result, it may take you a while to locate a loan officer willing to work with you.

If you can't find a loan officer willing to do business with you, re-contact those who seemed most sympathetic or with whom you have the best rapport and ask each of them what you should do to get a loan. You may have to save more money as tangible proof of how serious you are about getting your finances back on track; you may have to increase your income; or you may simply have to wait until there is more distance between you and your financial problems.

When you meet with a loan officer

When you find a loan officer willing to meet with you, ask the officer to mail you a loan application. Save time by completing it and bring it to your initial meeting. Also bring along a copy of your current credit report so you can discuss it, provide explanations as necessary, and demonstrate that you have not had any recent problems with credit. Your meeting with the loan officer provides you an opportunity to begin building trust. Do whatever you can to ensure the officer that your financial problems will not recur and that today you're a good candidate for a loan. Explain how your life has changed since you got into financial trouble and/or what you have done to stabilize your financial situation. Remember, loan officers are inherently conservative and risk averse, so you need to convince them that you are a good risk. If your credit problems were the result of poor money management skills, tell the loan officer about the steps you've taken to develop better skills. If your money troubles developed because of problems in your life such as your spouse was laid off, you got a divorce, or you were ill and unable to work, explain how things have changed.

Should your first meeting go well, the loan officer will probably want to schedule a second meeting after ordering and reviewing another copy of your credit record. The officer will do this to be sure it does not reflect any reoccurring problems; that you have been forthcoming about all aspects of your financial history; and that you have not begun applying for a lot of new credit. If the officer seems reluctant to make the loan, even on a secured basis, ask what you need to do to get the loan you want.

If the loan officer approves you for cash secured loan, the loan will probably be for an amount close to what you have in your savings account. Most likely, you will be asked to put the loan proceeds in a certificate of deposit at the bank. You will also be expected to begin paying off the loan according to the terms of your loan agreement. Most likely, you have a year or so to complete your payments. Be sure to make each payment on time so that you prove to the loan officer you are serious about rebuilding your credit and so that the officer will be open to making you a loan that is not cash secured. Getting a second loan is important because it usually takes more than a positive payment history or just a single loan to rebuild damaged credit history.

Before getting a second loan after you have paid off your first loan, order a copy of your credit report from each of the big three credit bureaus. Make sure that each of the reports accurately reflects the history of your payments on the cash secured loan you just paid off. If one or more do not reflect that history, ask the loan officer if the bank will report your loan payment history to the other credit bureaus.

After your first loan has been paid in full, let the loan officer know that you want to apply for a second loan that is not cash secured. If you had no problem paying off your first loan, it should be easy to get this next loan. If you have trouble, however, go to another bank. Once you get a second loan, pay it off just like the first one, and after it's paid off, once again check your credit history with each of the big three.

Shopping for a credit card

Before applying for national secured bankcard, a Visa or MasterCard, take some time to understand the terminology and features of bank cards out there. Your goal should be to get the best deal. The best deal is not simply the bankcard with the highest credit limit; in fact, the credit limit should be one of the least important considerations. Because the first bankcard you apply for probably will be secured, your credit limit will depend on how much money you put up as security. Factors more important to consider when shopping for a bank card include an annual fee, interest rate, late payment fee, and grace period.

Secured or collateralized bank cards

Using a secured bankcard responsibly is an excellent way to build creditors trust in your ability to use new credit so that eventually you can get an unsecured card. Banks that issue secured cards require cardholders to secure or collateralized their credit purchases by opening a savings account with them or by purchasing a CD from them. That way, if you don't pay your secured bankcard debt, the bank can get repaid by withdrawing the money you owe on your savings account or by cashing in your CD. On the other hand, if you make your secured bankcard payments in full and on time each month, the bank will not need to tap your collateral and your payment history will gradually improve. Eventually, depending on your payment history, you may be able to obtain a regular bankcard.

Once you have a secured bankcard

Once you have a secured national bankcard, use it to charge only necessities, not something frivolous that you would normally buy with cash. Put aside the cash amount of your charged purchases so that you'll have the money you need to pay your bankcard bill when it arrives. After you have used your card for six months, order a copy of your credit record from each of the big three to make certain your account payments are now a part of your credit history.

Be wary of carrying over your account balance from month to month. Doing so can make it easy to run up a big balance that you may be unable to pay-and carrying a balance from month to month is expensive.

When evaluating secured bankcard offers, one of your primary goals should be to find a bankcard issuer that reports to at least one of the big three. Ideally, however, the bank that issued you a bankcard reports to all of them. If it reports to just one, the credit rebuilding process will take a lot longer.

Month 7

Continue paying bills on time and in full. Delinquent payments can have a major negative impact on your score and the longer you pay your bills on time, the better your score. For example, someone with an average credit rating of 707 can raise their score by as much as 20 points by paying all their bills on time for one month.

Insider Secret

Request a credit limit increase with no intention of using it.

Some "experts" will lead you to believe that you must pay down debts using your cash in order to see an immediate reduction in your debt to available balance ratio. However, instead of using up your much needed cash, pick up the phone and call the credit card companies and request a limit increase. If they approve it, your ratios will greatly improve without having paid a cent towards your balance!

Six

What is a credit repair company?

Although some credit repair firms are legitimate businesses that work within the law to help consumers resolve credit record problems and rebuild their credit, most credit repair firms charge exorbitant fees- anywhere between $50-$2000 to correct a consumer's credit record. They claim that they can make bad credit, even bankruptcies, disappear from the consumer's credit record. Some of these firms are little more than floating con artists. They move into a location, charge unsuspecting consumers a hefty upfront fee for their services, and then skip town, leaving their victims poor and without the credit record improvements that they were promised.

Credit repair companies cannot do anything you can't do yourself for little or no cost under the terms of the FCRA.

That law gives you the right to have inaccurate or outdated information deleted from your credit record and to have written statements inserted in your credit record.

Neither you nor a credit repair firm can remove certain types of information from your credit record until the law allows their removal. The FCRA allows most negative information to remain in your credit record for seven years, although bankruptcies may be reported for up to 10 years, they too can sometimes be removed early. Credit repair companies can't change the law for their clients. Only time can erase negative information on your credit record unless the negative information is erroneous.

How to spot a fraudulent credit repair company

Some illegitimate credit repair firms are easy to spot; others can be more difficult to identify because they may market themselves as financial counseling and advice companies. To prevent your being duped, the following are sure signs of a credit repair company that will rip you off:

1. The company makes impossibly extravagant promises about what it can do for you, such as: "we can wipe out bankruptcies and other negative information, no matter how bad your credit history."

2. The company says it will use little-known loopholes in the FCRA to rid credit record of negative information.

3. The company claims that it can get you a major bankcard despite your credit record.

Use a wide variety of techniques to market their services to consumers. These techniques may include distributing fliers in parking lots and posting them on telephone poles, advertising on television, using direct mail, telemarketing, and sending e-mail messages to consumers. Credit repair firms that use direct mail or telemarketing to market their services often develop their target list of consumers from court records of people who have filed for bankruptcy.

No matter how a credit repair firm tries to reach you, its goal is to get you to learn more about its services or to schedule an appointment with the credit repair firm representative. The firm knows that if you are anxious to get rid of negative information in your credit file, you may fall for the promises of its representative. To help you separate fact from fiction so that you will be less apt to fall for empty promises, listed below are three of the most common claims a credit repair firm makes when they are marketing their services to desperate consumers:

Products and services of credit repair firms

In addition to their credit repair services, some credit repair firms also offer debt consolidation loans, debt counseling services, and national bankcards. Their loans, however, often come with very high interest rates and substantial upfront fees. Borrowers may also have to post their home as collateral; and sometimes a scamming credit repair firm will misrepresent the terms of the collateralized loan, making consumers vulnerable to the loss of their home.

The debt counseling services of credit repair firms often consist of recommending bankruptcy when bankruptcy is not a consumer's best option. Typically their offer for national bankcards is nothing more than an application for a secured bankcard, something you can obtain on your own.

Credit repair company techniques

To fix problems in your credit record, these so called reputable credit repair companies may use techniques that are illegal or questionable at best. If you make a false statement on a loan or credit application, misrepresent your Social Security number, or obtain an EIN from the IRS under false pretenses, all things that a credit repair firm may ask you to do, you will be committing a federal crime and subject to prosecution. Therefore, it is very important that you understand the kind of fix it techniques credit repair firms commonly use so that if a company's advertising doesn't tip you off that the company is a credit repair firm, its techniques will.

The use of loopholes

The FCRA gives you the right to challenge anything that you don't believe is accurate. If a credit reporting agency is unable to verify the disputed information within 30 days, it must immediately delete the information from your credit record.

Some credit repair firms try to abuse this provision of the law by flooding credit reporting agencies with numerous and repeated request to delete negative information in a consumers credit file. The credit repair firm doesn't care if some of the information it disputes is correct because it's strategy is to overwhelm the credit bureau with so many requests that it will be impossible for the credit bureau to verify all of the disputed information by the end of the 30 day deadline and the unverified information will have to be deleted, correct or not.

Credit bureaus have a number of defenses to use against this tactic. First, they can dismiss credit record information disputes that they consider to be frivolous or irrelevant. Second, they have decreased the amount of time it takes them to respond to disputed information by, for example, increasing their use of e-mail to communicate with the provider of the disputed information. Credit repair companies that are determined to victimize consumers, however, continued to figure out ways to manipulate the FCRA at the expense of consumers.

Quick-fix methods

A popular credit repair firm technique is to create a new, problem free credit identity for a consumer. Its objective is to hide the negative information in the consumer's credit file by tricking a credit bureaus computer.

One commonly used method for accomplishing such tricking is called file segregation, or skin shredding, an illegal technique, as mentioned earlier, that involves altering a consumer's credit file.

Typically, financially troubled consumers receive a letter or phone call from a credit repair firm telling them that for a fee the firm can help hide the negatives in their credit records and establish a new credit identity for them. The consumers are instructed to use their new identity when applying for credit in the future. Once consumers pay the fee, the credit repair firm will tell them to apply to the IRS for an EIN and to use it rather than their Social Security number whenever they apply for credit. An EIN and resembles a Social Security number and is used by businesses to report information to the IRS and the Social Security Administration. Consumers will also be instructed to use a new mailing address on the credit applications.

Another tactic used by some credit repair firms is to advise their clients to send a check for a partial payment of a past due account and to write on the check that by cashing it the creditor agrees to cease all collection activity and to delete all negative information related to that account from the consumers credit file. However, creditors are not legally required to such terms of payment and, furthermore, if a creditor excepted the terms, the consumer would have to take additional steps to ensure that the terms of payment were actually met. That's because it is unlikely that the credit repair firm would do the necessary follow-up, thereby leaving the consumer more in debt from having paid money to both the creditor and the credit repair firm-and with the problem the consumer was trying to erase still on his or her credit file.

As this chapter has already made quite clear, quick-fix credit repair methods are not recommended because they are morally questionable and often illegal as well. Furthermore, if credit repair firms successfully erase bad credit from consumer files or create a new identity for consumers, they may be helping consumers obtain new credit before the consumers have had an opportunity to put their money problems in perspective, to understand why the problems occurred, and to acquire better money management skills. As a result, those consumers are apt to repeat their mistakes and end up in serious financial trouble again in the future.

How to find a reputable credit repair firm

If you'd like to have a credit repair firm help you deal with problems in your credit record because you lack confidence that you can do it yourself or you don't have the time, use caution when trying to determine a good firm from a bad one. I personally recommend Lexington Law Firm (lexingtonlaw. com). Over the years they have helped me and others without any incidents.

Month 8

Minimize your debt-to-income ratio. Your debt-to-income ratio is the measure of how much debt you carry to how much money (after taxes) you have coming in. In the world of banking, it is acceptable to carry 25% of your income in debt. Some may say that ratio is too high. At the very least you should keep your debt to 15% or less of your after-tax income (including home & auto loans).

Insider Secret
Report your credit cards lost.

With the goal of adding an additional positive trade line without applying anywhere or even if you don't qualify, simply call your creditor and report your credit card lost or stolen. When this happens, they will usually close that account and open a new account, issue you a new card with a new number while transferring all of your positive credit history over to the new account including the original open date. Bam! You now have two positive and seasoned credit lines just like that.

Seven

CREATING DIVORCE -PROOF CREDIT

Planning For a Divorce

If you are contemplating divorce, be sure to minimize any potential financial damage that the change in marital status may cause by taking certain steps before filing. These steps include the following:

1. Know the status of the accounts you and your spouse are currently using. Are they joint, authorized-user, or individual? Is each account current?

2. Make sure you have established credit in your own name. If you have not, delay your divorce if possible until you can get some individual credit and open a bank account in your own name.

3. If you currently have joint or individual credit, obtain a copy of your credit report from each of the

big three and address any problems you may find in them.

4. If some of the accounts in your credit file are joint accounts with negative histories, and if the adverse information is the fault of your soon-to-be former spouse or the result of circumstances beyond your control, prepare a written explanation of the reason(s) for the negative information and ask the credit bureau to make this explanation a permanent part of your credit history. Doing so may help disassociate you from the account's problems. It is also a good idea to attach the same explanation to any credit applications you complete.

5. Pay all bills and credit card debts you share with your spouse from your joint funds. Then send a letter to each creditor canceling the cards. If you leave the accounts open, you risk being liable for the balances on the accounts.

6. If you have a lawyer or a financial adviser, talk with that person about what you should do to prepare for the change in your marital status.

7. If your spouse files for bankruptcy while you are in the process of divorce, it is likely that the divorce, proceedings will be stopped until the bankruptcy is completed, or the automatic stay will be lifted so your divorce can proceed. During this time, talk with your lawyer about how to minimize the impact of your spouse's troubles on your financial situation.

Avoiding Trouble with Joint Accounts

Creditors consider spouses with joint accounts, including loans, credit cards, lines of credit, and so on, to be equally liable for those accounts. It is critical that you close all joint accounts as soon as possible and reopen new accounts separately in your own name; authorized-user accounts should be closed. If you do not close these accounts, you risk being liable for any charges incurred by your now ex-spouse even if your divorce agreement says your former spouse will be responsible for the accounts. Because your name is still on the accounts, you are still legally liable from a creditor's point of view. Furthermore, if your ex-spouse is late making payments on the joint accounts or defaults on them, your credit record, not just your ex-spouse's, will be damaged, harming your ability to build a life for yourself as a single person.

Close joint accounts by writing to each creditor. If there is an outstanding balance on an account, ask that the balance be transferred to the new individual account of whichever spouse will be responsible for paying off the account according to your divorce agreement. Also ask that the spouse who is not responsible be released from liability for the account. Although the creditor is not obligated to do what you have requested, it is important that you and your spouse are clear about who will be responsible for each debt after you are divorced.

If at all possible, avoid negotiating a divorce agreement that allows your spouse to maintain your joint accounts in exchange for paying off the outstanding balances on these accounts. As long as these joint accounts remain open, you will be legally responsible for them regardless of what your divorce agreement provides.

Debts That Your Spouse Agrees to Pay as Part of Your Divorce Settlement

When you decide to get divorced, part of your divorce negotiations will involve deciding how to divide your marital debts as well as your assets. These decisions should be clearly outlined in your divorce agreement. Send a letter to each of the creditors affected by your agreement notifying them of what you and your spouse have decided.

After your divorce, you are expected to pay off the debts for which you assumed responsibility. However, if your spouse fails to pay a particular creditor, the creditor can seek payment from you if your name was originally on the account when the debt was first incurred. If you decide to take back your maiden name after your divorce, be certain to inform your creditors. Ask them to report account information to credit bureaus under your new name. Periodically check your credit report afterwards to make sure your creditors are reporting the correct information to the credit bureaus.

Month 9

Limit hard inquiries- While they won't destroy you, hard inquiries can slightly lower your score so apply for new accounts with caution. Keep in mind that applying for a credit card is not the only way to receive a hard inquiry. Getting a cell phone, applying for cable services, or opening a bank account may result in a credit inquiry.

Insider Secret
Become an authorized user on someone else's credit card

The most efficient way to increase your credit score in a short time is by becoming an authorized user on someone else's credit card. Once you become authorized, the new positive trade line will show up on your credit as if you've had it from day one. It is really important that you only attach yourself to a long standing credit line that has only positive information. Additionally, it should be someone you trust and vice versa because if the primary user runs up big debt, has late payments, or defaults, you could be held responsible and your credit will certainly be damaged!

Eight

Today, personal details about your life can be accessed with a mere push of a button. In fact, just about anything is available for sale, including your employment history, medical records, marital status and details about where you live. Several companies maintain thousands of different databases developed from a wide variety of public records, including birth and wedding announcements, telephone directories, voter registration records, motor vehicle records, and court filings.

Often times the information in one database is combined with information from another to create marketable new information products or to improve existing databases. In other situations, information from one database may be compared with that of another to help identify consumers with particular characteristics or to make an existing database more comprehensive and accurate. Databases are also being linked electronically to create huge information networks.

Personal information has become a valuable commodity. Yet the majority of the time we are unaware that the information about our finances, personal habits, health, buying patterns, and other such information is being bought, sold, and exchanged, nor are we aware as to where that information originates from. Even worse, there is little that can be done to stop what is happening with our personal information.

Unauthorized Access and Use of Credit Report Data

Unauthorized access to consumer credit files is easily obtained, especially now that online access is available from all major credit bureaus. Some businesses are misrepresenting themselves to gain access to credit bureau data. In some instances those who have a legitimate reason to access credit record data are using that information for illegal purposes in violation of federal law or are selling it to others for unauthorized uses.

Although recent changes to the FCRA attempt to restrict who has access to credit record data, there is no reason to believe the problem will stop, considering the huge earnings potential that businesses and individuals can realize from consumer credit record data. Credit bureaus do not adequately police what their subscribers do with the consumer credit information in their files once they have it. Although laws are in place to minimize problems, the potential for fraud remains.

Federal Privacy Laws

Today, some of the most personal details of your life are being searched through and seized using technology rather than by physical means. As a result, most of the federal privacy laws that currently exist, including the FCRA, are inadequate. Not only are these laws outdated, but many are full of loopholes and exemptions that make them easy to bypass. In addition to the FCRA, the most significant federal privacy laws are the Privacy Act of 1974, the Right to Financial Privacy Act of 1978, the Video Privacy Protection Act, and the Computer Matching and Privacy Protection Act.

The Privacy Act of 1974

The privacy act of 1974 applies to federal agencies, prohibiting them from obtaining data for one purpose and then using it for another. The exception to the law applies when information is shared for "routine use," which essentially makes the law useless because any use can be interpreted as "routine".

The Right to Financial Privacy Act

Even though the Right to Financial Privacy Act is supposed to govern access of federal agencies to your bank records, exemptions allow U.S. attorneys and the FBI to review bank records. This law also does not apply to private employers or to local and state governments. Furthermore, new exceptions are added to this law annually, continuously limiting the power of the law to truly protect your financial privacy.

The Video Privacy Protection Act

The Video Privacy Protection Act prohibits retailers from providing a list of the videos you rent unless you approve the release of that information or a court order is issued ordering the release.

The Computer Matching and Privacy Protection Act

The Computer Matching and Privacy Protection Act regulates the federal governments use of computer matching techniques that compare information in one computer file to data in another to determine your eligibility for federal benefits. The law also limits the federal government's use of matching techniques to help it collect money, such as taxes. The law does not apply to all entities who may conduct potential matches, including matches done for law enforcement purposes.

Prescreening

Prescreening is a process by which a credit bureau creates a list of consumers qualified to receive a preapproved offer of credit using the information in its credit files. Prescreening can be done in one of two ways. First, a company may supply a credit bureau with a set of credit granting characteristics that describe its target market. For example, a credit card company may want to offer a preapproved card to all consumers who make over $100,000 a year and have flawless credit records and several lines of unused credit.

The credit bureau doing the prescreening will compare the criteria specified by the credit card company with characteristics of the consumers in its database. From this comparison, a list of prescreened consumers will be created for the credit card company to market its offer to.

A company may also provide a credit bureau with a list of criteria defining the types of consumers to whom it wants to market to, The credit bureau will then compare the information it has in its database with the criteria the creditor has specified in order to identify who should receive that company's offer.

The practice of prescreening if often criticized because it is done without the knowledge of consumers. Even though the company that purchases the prescreened list does not actually view the credit files of the consumers on the list, concern exists because technology has helped credit bureaus refine the criteria that can be used in the prescreening process. As a result, companies can now obtain specific details about your financial life without ever seeing your credit history.

Month 10

Maintain Discipline- Have credit cards but manage them responsibly. In general, having credit cards and installment loans (and making timely payments) will raise your score. Someone with no credit cards, for example, tends to be higher risk than someone who has managed credit cards responsibly.

Nine

Maintaining your Credit

Once you have started to rebuild your credit and your financial troubles began to disappear, you may be tempted to continue some of the bad habits which caused you to get into financial trouble and damage your credit in the first place. Habits to avoid may include:

1. Applying for and using to many credit cards
2. Running up the balance on any open lines of credit
3. Frequently using ATM or debit cards and failing to put money in your account on a regular basis

If you happen to find yourself performing old bad habits, try your best to stop and think about the risks of your actions. Recovering from serious financial problems, even bankruptcy, is difficult enough the first time but can even be more of a disaster the second time around because most creditors will feel you didn't learn your lesson and therefore be unwilling to extend credit to you again.

The key to keeping your spending under control may be to create a budget. Make sure your plan is realistic and stick to it. A budget will allow you to allocate your income so that you are able to meet your monthly obligations. Any additional money left over can be placed into a savings account. If no additional money is left over, you may want to consider seeking a second job. Building a savings will help to reduce your use of credit.

If you have difficulty controlling your spending, you may have emotional issues relating to money. Consider speaking with a psychologist in order to help you understand and over-come your inability to handle money.

Too many may be too much

Avoid having to many credit cards at one time. One or two major credit cards, perhaps one emergency or travel card, and possibly a gasoline card are all you need. Avoid department store and retail cards, which carry unreasonably high interest rates. Most all retailers accept Visa and MasterCard.

Having lots of credit cards may cause you to become tempted to use them. Furthermore, some creditors consider it to be more of a risk if they know you have access to several lines of credit even if you rarely use them or have no balance. Creditors know that at any time you have the potential to begin using them.

Regardless of what you may hear, it is a good idea to close all credit cards except for those you absolutely need even if you still owe a balance. The credit cards that offer you the least beneficial terms should be eliminated. Make sure the accounts you are closing do not have an acceleration clause, which may allow the card issuer to demand payment in full upon closing your account.

Traits of a Good Debtor

Though it is important to limit the number of credit cards you have, it is equally as important to monitor how much credit you have compared to your monthly income especially if you plan to never again have financial troubles. Even overuse of one credit card can cause you to develop financial hardship.

When applying for credit, the creditor will compare the amount of credit you have to your income. If that ratio is too high, even if you have a substantial income, you may encounter difficulty obtaining credit at satisfactory terms. A simple way to figure out if you have too much debt relative to your income is to compare your financial situation to what is considered standard appropriate or safe debt to income ratios. If your ratios exceed the standards, then you should immediately reduce your debt. The ratios you should compare yourself to should be somewhere along the following lines:

Your debt to income ratio for credit cards and loans is your total monthly credit payments divided by your total income

If your debt to income ratio is under 20 percent, you are doing well. The lower the better; 10 percent or less is always ideal.

If your ratio is over 20 percent, reduce spending; stop the use of credit cards and focus on paying down your card balances.

If your ratio exceeds 35 percent, you are nearing an unsatisfactory level. Although some creditors will still work with you, it is unlikely that you will be eligible for offers with the most favorable terms.

Next is the ratio of your mortgage payment to your monthly gross income. When reviewing a mortgage loan application, banks generally like to see a ratio in the range of 28 to 36 percent. If your ration is high than that, you may be asked to come up with a larger down payment or pay a higher interest rate.

What Creditors Want To See

When you apply for a bank loan, the bank will evaluate your creditworthiness using capacity, capital, and character (also known as the three C's).

Capacity- Do you as a borrower have the capacity to re-pay the loan? To determine this, a creditor will look at the ratios described previously, your income, your payment history, and your employment history.

Capital- Do you have any assets that can be used as collateral to cover the credit you are asking for? Creditors like to see collateral even if you are applying for unsecured credit because they want to be sure you have assets to cover any debts if you fail to pay. If you do not possess any assets, you may be unable to obtain the credit you want, or the credit will be granted to you with unfavorable terms.

Character- Are you trustworthy? The creditor will make this assessment based on your past payment history with others creditors. They may also consider your history of paying rent, utilities, and phone bills.

Types of Credit

When you apply for a bank loan or credit card, chances are you will be applying for a revolving, open-end, or an open 30-day account.

Revolving or Open-End Accounts

If your credit account is revolving or open-end, you will have a fixed amount of credit that you will not be expected to exceed. Each month you will have to at least pay the minimum amount due on the account, which will likely be a percentage of the total amount you owe. Examples of revolving credit include *Visa*, *MasterCard* or any secured bank cards.

Installment or Closed-End Accounts

For this type of credit, you will borrow a set amount of money and be expected to pay it back in set amounts over a predetermined period of time. Examples of this type of credit include bank installment loans, where your monthly payment will likely include principal and interest, and also mortgage loans, which are usually stretched out over many years. The property you mortgage will serve as collateral in case you default.

Open 30-Day Credit Accounts

With this type of account you can charge up to a certain credit limit but must pay off the entire balance each month or within 30 days of the billing date. Examples of this type of credit are retail or department store cards, gas cards, and travel cards like American Express.

Evaluating Offers of Credit

Almost every day, your mailbox is flooded with credit card offers. Some offer low interest rates while others offer no annual fee and free balance transfers. Before making a decision you should consider how you will be using the card. Ask yourself what types of benefits you need. Will you be paying the balance off in full each month?

Credit Card Traps

Solicitations from credit card providers may sound attractive until you read the details of the offer. Most offers are actually bad for consumers and good for the credit card company because they generate tons of money at your expense. Some things to watch for when looking for a new credit card include the following:

- High annual fees or annual fees that escalate after a period of time
- Penalties for making on time payments or not using your card regularly.
- Offers that lure you in with a super low rate and encourage transferring a balance from one card over to another card with a lower rate. Often times, the initial low rate will last for only a short period of time then rise to a much higher rate.
- Increases in your annual rate if you exceed your credit limit or fail to make a payment on time.

- Immediate fees for being late with a payment or exceeding your credit limit.

There is no need to wait for credit card offers to be mailed to you. If you know of a card with favorable terms, contact the card issuer to submit an application. If you currently have a credit card with unattractive terms, consider asking the card issuer to revise the terms of your current agreement to meet or exceed other offers you have received. If you have a good payment history, the credit card company may be willing to work with you rather than lose you as a customer.

Month 11

Be patient- You will not build good credit overnight. Whether you are waiting for derogatory marks to be deleted from your report or simply waiting for your average age of accounts to rise, there is nothing you can do to speed up time.

Ten

This chapter was created for the majority of people who are impatient or lacking the time necessary to read this or any other book from front to back. Sometimes you just want to get to the point and be done. Some of us enjoy reading and have the ability to easily comprehend or understand the message outlined in a book. For others, it takes a little longer to catch on.

For those of you who are not familiar with my background, I started off with absolutely no credit and in less than a year I had built an average FICO score of 730. I purchased tons of stuff using credit and got myself into a jam which resulted in me filing bankruptcy. After the bankruptcy my credit score hit an all-time low of 487. I couldn't get anything on credit if my life depended on it. I needed to find a way to bounce back. I began researching credit repair methods and different strategies used to build credit. Mistakes were made along the way but eventually through trial and error, I was able to get my credit score to 771 within 12 months. If you currently have terrible credit I want you to fully understand that I too was once there. I know exactly what it is like and I know what it takes to recover. Often times you will hear other people give advice on how to rebuild credit. My advice to you is to never take advice from someone who has not walked in your shoes and never take advice from someone who has not been where you are trying to go.

If your credit is greatly blemished and you don't have a clue where to begin, I'm about to break down to you very specific steps you can apply TODAY! That's right. Not later on. Not next month. Not next year. TODAY! It has been said that "Anything the mind can conceive it can achieve". While that sounds good, at the end of the day the only thing that will move you in the right direction is ACTION. Reading this book then doing absolutely nothing will have absolutely no positive effect on your credit score. You must prepare and follow through with consistent action in order to attain your goal. In my lifetime, I have been both up and down financially. During those times when I was down, this credit building method has ALWAYS greatly improved my credit score after a financial hardship. This method will also work for you just as it has for me but only if you exercise patience and discipline.

If you have not retained any information from this entire book its ok. The following steps will advance you much further than chapters 1-9 combined. I want to extend my personal guarantee that if you complete these steps as mentioned, your credit score and financial well-being overall will be forever changed.

Step 1- In order to carry out this plan you must have at least $1000. Some of the steps can be completed with less money but I personally recommend having $1000 or more to maximize your overall success. I personally use a minimum of $2000-$5000. If you do not have $1000 at your disposal, attempt to get it. If for whatever reason you are unable to get $1000, I will later explain how you can still benefit from this method.

Step 2- Find a bank or credit union that is willing to give you a secured loan using your bank account or deposit as collateral. If you are confused with this step, simply call or go to your local bank and ask to speak with a personal banker or representative. Explain to the banker that you are looking to obtain a secured loan and that you have $1000 that you are willing to deposit and use as collateral. If the bank does handle this type of loan, the banker will then explain 1 of 2 options. The first option will be for you to purchase a certificate of deposit (CD) using your $1000 and then allow the bank to use your newly purchased CD as collateral. In return the bank will then give you a loan in the amount of $1000 which you will then make monthly payments on based on terms agreed upon by you and the bank. Option 2 would be to open a savings account at the bank by depositing your $1000 and allowing them to "freeze" the money while issuing you a loan for the same amount.

Step 3- Once you have received your $1000 loan, you will then take the proceeds and repeat the exact same process again this time using a different bank.

Before applying for any of these loans make sure that the banks or lending institutions that you choose report consumer payment history to at least 1 if not all 3 of the major credit bureaus. This is essential in order to build your credit score.

Now your credit report will show that you currently have two secured installment loans totaling $2000 (2 loans x $1000 each)

Pay Close Attention:

Repeat Step 3 once again using yet again another bank or lending institution. As you are in the process of completing these steps stay focused and DO NOT spend any of the loan proceeds.

Wait a minute…. In case I lost you during any of these steps lets go over things.

You started off with $1000 in cash. You went to 3 different banks or lending institutions and you now have 3 separate loans for $1000 each. You also have payments which are due monthly on each loan. These payments (even with high interest rates) should total no more than $50 each if you stretch them over 24 months. **Don't worry about the 24 month term because you will pay the loans off early** (within 3-10 months). The term is simply stretched out so that the monthly payments will be smaller.

Step 4- Now is not the time to screw this up. Make your payments on time for each loan. I know what you are thinking. You've just created 3 additional bills every month totaling $150. This is certainly true but these payments are minimal in comparison to what you will achieve overall by completing this method.

As stated earlier, do not spend the loan proceeds. I understand that this may be difficult for some people especially if money is tight but you must demonstrate discipline. Try to make the payments using your income just as you would your normal bills. You must **MAKE PAYMENTS FOR AT LEAST 3 MONTHS**. Do this **6-10 months for optimal results.**

NOTE: Regardless of what you may think or what others may say, using this method for just 3 months will produce results. Several bankers and loan officers have often doubted my methods over the years. Now those same individuals consult with me when they have clients with troubled credit. Once again, never take advice from people who have not been in your position.

Pay Close Attention:

Step 5- After enough time has passed (3-10 months), you will then take the $1000 proceeds received from your 3rd loan and completely pay off your 1st loan. Once your 1st loan is paid off, the bank or lending institution will then release your collateral ($1000). You will then use those proceeds to completely pay off your 2nd loan. Again, the bank or lending institution will release their lien on your collateral ($1000). You guessed it! You will then use the $1000 from the 2nd loan to completely pay off your 3rd and final loan.

NOTE: When you go to pay off your loans in full, the total balance owed on each loan will be less than $1000 because you have been making regular principal and interest payments which resulted in a decrease of the overall balance. Therefore, do not be surprised if you have a few hundred dollars left over after paying off each loan. (Spend it wisely).

Your credit report will reflect the following:

You initially took out 3 loans at 3 different banks or lending institutions totaling $3000 (3 loans x $1000 each).

You have now not only paid off all three loans but you have done so much earlier than the terms you originally agreed to. During my personal experience, each time I have paid off a secured loan early, the bank will often offer an unsecured loan in the same amount if not greater. By going to multiple banks to obtain loans you have began to build a business relationship with each of them. Also by having obtained loans from multiple sources, you have broadened your credit report by showing you are capable of having multiple loans from multiple banks at the same time and that you were responsible enough to not only pay them all off but you did so much earlier than expected. The following month after completing this method I guarantee your credit score will greatly improve.

That's not all…

If you are serious about improving credit quickly, you can also use this exact same method with secured credit cards while at the same time having secured loans. **Using this method for both installment loans and credit cards at the same time will push your credit score through the stratosphere!**

For those of you who can not come up with the $1000 to complete the installment loan method, the credit card method is perfect for you.

Secured credit cards can be obtained using as little as $200. The method is exactly the same as with installment loans. The only difference is instead of receiving a loan for your secured collateral, you will now be receiving a credit card with a limit equal to the amount you submit for collateral.

By all means, if you can afford to do both the installment loan method along with the credit card method your score will rapidly increase.

These 2 methods when properly executed will create positive credit history and help to display a versatile credit profile satisfactory to most banks, credit card companies and lending institutions.

Month 12

Rinse & repeat- Fancy maneuvers are not necessary to keep your credit looking good. Simply keep your spending under control, pay your bills on time, and don't apply for extra credit too often. In no time you will find yourself among those with elite credit-score status!

In Closing...

I would like to send my thanks to you for taking the time to allow me to spread some of the wealth of information I have accumulated over the years. Hopefully I have provided you with beneficial knowledge you may use and share with others for many years to come. I appreciate life and will continue helping others for as long as I can. I only ask that you yourself do the same. Peace, love, and happiness to all.

'0920621R00064

Made in the USA
Middletown, DE
18 April 2018